Barbara Stieff

Earth, Sea, Sun, and Sky

Art in nature

PRESTEL
Munich · London · New York

Content

Look for these clues

A Grove of ever greens

A Temple of View

Cabinet

Cabinet

Fruit Garden

Flower garden

An open plaun of Grass

Aromatick Herbs as Cammomile &c.

Physick garden

Slip Garden

T. Inskley Sculp.

I. Langley Delin.

I. Langley Invent.

Small Paradises
and Great Art

When we speak of nature, we mean everything that's simply there – the mountains and the sea, the plants and animals. But art, in contrast, comes about only through the imagination and creativity of people. But how do they fit together?

People began giving nature an artistic form very early in history.
They designed gardens where they could stroll, relax, and play. Using buckets and spades, gardeners have built both small and large paradises.

During the last century, artists found a completely new way to deal with nature: Land Art. Even today, they are still searching for new ways to work in and with nature. Some dig it up with giant earthmovers, and others wrap it up like a present. Some want to use art to delve into the secret of life and nature.

In this book, not only can you read about what these artists did and look at the amazing pictures, but you can get active yourself. There are many games and ideas that will inspire you to look at art and nature through the eyes of an artist. Are you ready?

Nature

As soon as the weather permits, there's only one thing on many people's minds: getting out into nature. Outdoors, you can romp and frolic around to your heart's content. There's plenty of room to cruise around on your bike. You can hide in the foliage, build sand castles or dams, go hiking or swimming, or just lie happily under a tree and daydream.

Since nature is an important part of this book, it makes sense to ask what we mean when we speak of nature. What is part of nature? Surely it includes plants, animals, mountains, valleys, rivers, lakes, and the ocean. Are air and the weather part of nature, too? What do you think? How about the sky and the sun, moon, and stars? Or is nature only on the Earth?

If you'd like to build up your strength for the long journey in nature, here's a special recipe.

Read about it on page 80!

Scientists have defined nature as that which has not been made by people, that is, what would still be here if there were no people. They distinguish between animate nature and inanimate nature. Animate nature includes everything that is alive, such as animals and plants. Inanimate nature would include, for example, rocks, water, or air.

Before the universe began, everything that exists - EVERYTHING - was compressed into a single, miniscule point. But suddenly - and no one knows why - the tiny point began to explode in size, like a kernel of popcorn in the heat: pop! This moment is called the Big Bang. The elements were set free and raced through space at an incomprehensible speed for billions of years. At some point, they slowed down, cooled off, and began to clump together into the heavenly bodies - into stars and planets. Our Earth ended up in a perfect place for life to develop. If Earth had been a little closer or a little further from the sun, life wouldn't have happened.

Talk about a happy ending!

When a little red ladybug crawls along your leg and tickles you, or the scent of flowers wafts through the air, nature seems friendly. It can be gentle, like a breeze or a flower bud. It can be fragile like thin ice, a spider's web, or a newborn baby. But when the sky thunders and lightening flashes, or a great wave crashes over you on the sea, nature can also be frightening. In moments like these we experience nature's power. Think of volcanic eruptions, tsunamis, and earthquakes! In the desert nature is barren, and in the jungle it is pure abundance. Nature can wear an endless variety of masks.

What's that growing there?

If you'd like to study the diversity of nature like a natural scientist, then choose a small piece of field, about three feet on each side, as a research plot. Look at your plot carefully and try to find as many different kinds of plants as possible. Take one of each kind, but be careful to avoid any protected species. At home, find a thick, heavy book and press the plants between the pages. You can find a nice empty scrapbook at the stationary store. When the plants are dry, glue them into your scrapbook and write their names next to them. If you don't know their names, look in books or on the Internet to find them out. If you would rather be more artistic, then you can make pretty collages with your pressed finds. Try gathering and pressing plants during different times of year so you can see how nature changes in your test plot.

Nature and life also have their own rhythm. That rhythm depends on the Earth's relation to the sun. Day and night exists because of the Earth's rotation. At the same time the Earth revolves around the sun; its orbit is sometimes closer and sometimes further away from the sun. This is why we have the seasons spring, summer, fall, and winter.

People's lives are often very hectic. We have to dash to an appointment, hurry to finish our homework, run to the store to pick something up, quickly get dressed, or rush to get somewhere. In nature things are a bit more calm. Everything takes its time. Things develop, grow, and flourish. Just think how long it takes from when you plant a seed until you see the first green shoots.

If you can't wait, there are beans that grow as swiftly as an arrow.

Read about it
on page 80!

Dying is also part of the cycle of life, of course. Life is a constant cycle of growth, flowering, maturity, bearing fruit, and decaying. Ultimately everything that lives also dies, when its time comes. In winter it is often hard for us to see the life in nature. The plants dry up. Just before the leaves fall from the trees, they take on beautiful colors. Then they decay on the ground and are transformed into humus, or nutrients for the soil. But there's still life beneath the surface. When the first warm rays of sun fall on the ground in spring, new leaves and flowers begin to grown again.

A Winter Dream

When the plants are covered by snow in winter, it looks almost like they're sleeping. Maybe they're even dreaming. Can you imagine what they would dream about? Maybe a tree dreams of its blossoms and the buzzing sound of bees in them. Maybe its roots dream of the refreshing footbath they'll take when the ground is no longer frozen. If you like, you can write a story about the winter dreams of a plant or draw its dreams in the form of a comic strip.

Culture

Wow, just think how incredibly lucky we humans are...
On our planet, we have everything we need to live:
light, warmth, water, air, and land.
We are part of nature, for our body is made of the same
building blocks as everything else in nature. There are even
salts and metals in us. But the bulk of our body is composed
of water: at least sixty percent, more than half.

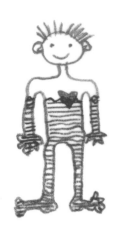

We are in constant interaction with our environment. Every day we
consume some of nature to nourish ourselves, and after digestion give
part of it back. Also when we breathe, nature becomes a part of us.
If we humans are part of nature and consist entirely of nature, then this
raises the question of why the things that we make are not nature?

Asking questions like these is call philosophizing. Feelings and
thoughts like these can make you curious and inspire you to look for
explanations. What could it be that separates us from nature?
What do you think?

Our lives are determined by nature. It gives us nourishment and raw materials with which
we can build houses, furniture, streets, tools, and machines… simply everything we need.
For we humans are clever, skillful, and inventive.

Through history, people have also tried to shape nature in different ways. The first way was agriculture. Stone-Age people discovered that it was possible to slightly tame the wildness of nature. They learned how to plant seeds, from which nourishing grain would grow a few months later. They began to cultivate the land. The first changes to nature were thus made for very practical reasons.

Over the course of many centuries, vegetable patches became fields, paths became streets and highways, simple settlements became villages and towns, clothing made of animal skins was replaced by suits and dresses, and so on. All these things are very practical and part of our life and our culture.

Forest path   Highway interchange in Shanghai, China

Ancient, Stone-Age peoples lived in houses   Skyscrapers in
like these, which stand on wooden stilts   Seattle, U.S.A.

In order to survive, early humans had to be very clever about how they interacted with nature. This is why during the Stone Age, people saw nature as something sacred. They wanted to make nature more mild and ask it for fertility. They tried to contact their nature gods through singing, dancing, and painting. Researchers have found giant wall paintings hidden deep inside caves. These are the the first works of art in the world.

Cave painting in Lascaux, France

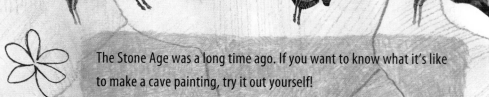

The Stone Age was a long time ago. If you want to know what it's like to make a cave painting, try it out yourself!

Read about it on page 81!

Gardens: Paradise on Earth

Not everything in life should only be practical. When your stomach is full, your work is done, and your room is picked up, you can do what you enjoy. Some people like to practice a musical instrument, read a book, play a game, get together with friends, do sports, or watch a film. When the earliest cultures had succeeded in taming nature, they began changing it for their pleasure.

Early History

During excavations in the Middle East, archaeologists found pictures and stone tablets telling about the first gardens, which existed many thousands of years ago. They were used for relaxation and enjoyment.

As early as 5,000 years ago, Sumerian soldiers (who lived in what is now Iraq) would find strange plants and animals on their military campaigns and bring them back home. There, these novelties were put in game preserves where people could admire and marvel at them. These were the first zoos and botanical gardens.

Imaginary plants

Not only nature can create amazing things, so can your imagination. Imagine that you have been on an exhibition in a distant land. There, you came across an unknown and very unusual plant. You wanted to bring it home with you, but unfortunately it didn't survive the long journey. So, in order for people to know what the plant is like, you'll have to draw it, cut it out of colored paper, or build it from modeling clay. What is unusual about this plant? Can it move or speak? Does it have giant flowers or some special healing power? Let your imagination take over. As the plant's discoverer, you can also choose its name!

Real gardens with beds developed when people learned how to irrigate. Old gravestones in Egypt show how well people were able to irrigate 4,500 years ago. Flowers and trees were shown in nice arrangements, with canals and pools in between them. Many of the pools were so large that small boats could even sail in them.

Egyptian wall painting of a garden, ca. 1400 B.C.

18

Around 2,600 years ago, King Nebuchadnezzar II had hanging gardens built for his wife Amyitis in Babylon, at the time a very large city. Supported by columns, lush green terraces rose up over the roofs of the city. It must have looked very impressive. The climate in this part of the world is very warm and dry, so the plants had to be watered often. It wasn't possible to use buckets to carry so much water so high up everyday, so the builders solved the problem by designing a pump. With the help of a jackscrew, they pumped the water from the Euphrates River all the way to the top of the gardens. This was a great technological achievement at the time. They made it possible for the most exquisite

Jackscrew

and rare plants to grow, bloom, and spread their scent in this site, surrounded by rocky desert. For the people of the time, this was a wonder; in fact, it was considered one of the seven wonders of the ancient world!

You too can amaze your friends with a little wonder. How?

Read about it on page 82!

These pictures show how we imagine the hanging gardens looked.

Ancient Greece and Rome

Many people in early history built impressive gardens for their rulers. More than 2,000 years ago, the Roman Empire learned from foreign cultures how to cultivate and irrigate plants. To make their gigantic parks, the whole area first had to be dug up, raised up, and changed. Hills arose where it had been flat before and ponds were built where everything had been dry and barren. These huge parks were open and spread out over several terraces. Shady palces stood next to sunny places. The environment became a stage, filled with plants, on which people met each other. People amused themselves with labyrinths and water games.

Small peristyle in the Getty Museum, reconstruction based on the Villa of the Papiri near Herculaneum, Italy

In the cities of the time, the gardens were smaller and surrounded by walls. House and garden were planned so skillfully that nature became a part of the house and vice versa. Like the Greeks had done before them, the Romans also beautified their gardens with fountains and statues. The statues depicted the gods to which the people prayed.

One special feature at the time was the public park. Here even simple craftsmen and poorer people could stroll along the paths and cool down in summer in the manmade springs and grottos (caves).

Garden of an ancient Roman house in Pompeii, 1st century A.D.

Middle Ages

The Middle Ages, which began about 1,500 years ago, were the times of knights and castles. Christianity and the Bible had spread through Europe. The first part of the Bible, the Old Testament, explains how God created the world in seven days.

This picture from a medieval book shows the creation of the world. The circle is meant to symbolize how God brings order to chaos.

> "And the Lord God planted a garden in Eden, in the East; and there he put the man whom he had formed. And out of the ground the Lord God made to grow every tree that is pleasant to the sight and good for food." (Genesis 2:8–9)

People imagined the paradise of the Bible to have been a wonderful place with a wall or fence around it, and they even named it the "Garden of Eden."

Would you also like to design a little paradise?

Read about it on page 82!

Many words are new, like google or supermarket. But other words have been around for a long, long time. The word "paradise" is ancient. It was already used in the ancient Persian language many thousands of years ago. Back then it looked a little bit different than it does today, namely like pairidaeza. Pairi means "all around" and daeza means "wall." Hmm … so paradise means a place with a wall around it.

This word pairidaeza was later translated into Greek as paradeisos. When it's written like this, it's actually pretty close to our word paradise, don't you think?

For the people of the Middle Ages, Eden was the most wonderful place on Earth. A perfect world filled with the peace, abundance, and eternal youth that they desired.

For their bleak life on Earth was not at all like paradise. In the enclosed courtyards of church cloisters, nuns and monks would stroll in silent prayer. The undecorated patch of grass in the courtyard was supposed to remind the faithful that paradise awaited them only in heaven.

Cloister courtyard

The gardens of the kings and nobles, in contrast, were very different. Surrounded by walls or fences to keep out animals and thieves, these were the first pleasure gardens. People could stroll through arcades filled with roses, listen to the birdsong, rest on grassy benches, and enjoy the small springs and ponds.

People could play chess with a friend in the shade of the trees, sing a love song, or try not to get lost in the mazes that had been laid out on the grounds. The garden was meant to be a place of delight that appealed to all the senses: seeing, smelling, feeling, tasting, hearing. Beds of herbs were planted just for their scent, and the air was filled with the mingling scents of sage, basil, savory, rosemary, lavender, and mint.

Medieval image by a German artist known as Master E. S., 1400s

Scent puzzle

If you'd like, you can test out how good the noses of your friends or family members are. Collect several different natural materials that have a strong smell, like acacia flowers or roses, dried grass, pieces of bark, or mushrooms. Enclose each one in a clean jar so that it retains its scent. It's also important that no one can see what's inside the jars. So before you fill them, paint the jars black or put each material in a little cloth sack beforehand. Now you can start. Who's got the best nose?

If you like to make things and are good with your hands, you can make a fragrant picture out of spices.

Find out how on page 83!

Renaissance and Baroque

Around the end of the Middle Ages, about 600 years ago, people suddenly rediscovered the magnificent cultures of ancient Greece and Rome. People wanted to revive these cultures - have them be reborn, so to speak. The French word for rebirth is renaissance. And that's what this period is still called today.

Instead of the high walls and the narrow fences of medieval gardens, everything now was once again vast and open. The entire landscape was

Baroque garden from Venetian Pleasures, Antoine Watteau, 1718-1719

designed geometrically - exactly like ancient models. There were absolutely straight lines, right angles, protected hedges, and level terraces. In this way, art, mathematics, and nature were combined.

It was as if these gardens had been made for social gatherings. There were water festivals with boats on the lake and costume balls with fireworks.

The guests were entertained by musicians and actors, tricked by magicians, and teased by jesters. For parties like these, the gardens had to look impressive, for their owners definitely wanted to show off with them.

Monster figure in the Park of Monsters in Bomarzo, Italy

Garden at the Palace of Versailles in Versailles, France

This kind of garden design was cultivated and even carried to extremes in the period following the Renaissance, which is called the Baroque. Many of these gardens have survived to the present day. They are usually part of a palace.

Would you like to organize your own water games?

Read how to on page 84!

The English Landscape Garden

Landscape gardens were developed around 250 years ago in England. They were meant to look totally romantic and natural, almost like nature itself, only "better." In this way people sought to create a new kind of paradise. Gently curving, open meadows were crisscrossed by little streams, which you could cross on narrow bridges. You could walk along meandering paths behind lush bushes or a small group of trees. Amidst the greenery you could stumble upon picturesque ruins, almost like in fairy tales.

Nymphenburg
palace park,
Munich, Germany

Landscape park in
Pavlovsk, Russia

To maintain the illusion of "real" wide-open nature, no fences were
allowed. But how could people keep the sheep - the lawnmowers of
their day - from running off? They invented the ha ha. The animals
could not get over these ditches and people couldn't see them from
a distance. Pretty clever!

A ha ha is
made from
a small wall
and a ditch.

Labyrinths and Mazes

Mazes were a popular attraction in the gardens of earlier times. They were designed for the amusement of people who loved to visit them. You have probably heard of mazes or maybe even visited one. Mazes were a kind of garden in which people could wander around and lose their way. Many people also call them labyrinths.

But this is somewhat confusing. A labyrinth and a maze are actually two different things. In one you can get lost, and in the other you find your way again. Let's take a closer look.

Labyrinth

The labyrinth is very old and was well-known in many cultures. It looks like this:

Stone-Age
cave carving

Ancient silver coins
from Greece

On first sight, the paths seem confusing. But when you trace them with your finger, you'll surely notice what's unusual about them.

Start

Although it looks otherwise, there are actually no wrong turns here. The labyrinth is a single path and you can't make a mistake in it. It is a symbol of life. It teaches people to have trust.

Did you notice that in the beginning your finger was very close to the middle? And at the next turn it was suddenly further outside? Imagine this route is your path through life. Let's say the first segment of the labyrinth's path is the time before you started school. By the end of preschool you were one of the bigger kids and already more clever than the little ones. Maybe you were even allowed to play while the little ones still had to take a nap. And then came summer vacation - like a curve on the labyrinth's path - and then school. How did it feel to suddenly be one of the little ones again, starting again at the very beginning? On the labyrinth you have now arrived at a new segment: elementary school. The path seems to go backwards: in preschool you were one of the big kids, but in school you start again with the little ones. Yet if you keep going, making your way through many curves, you finally reach your goal.

Along the way you can look to the left and right and be happy about all the things you have experienced and already mastered.

Draw a labyrinth yourself

1. Draw a cross and four points on a sheet of paper.
≶ Fig.1

2. Moving in a clockwise direction, join each point to the next free one across from it. Your labyrinth is growing! ≶ Fig. 2-4

3. The labyrinth is done. ≶ Fig. 5

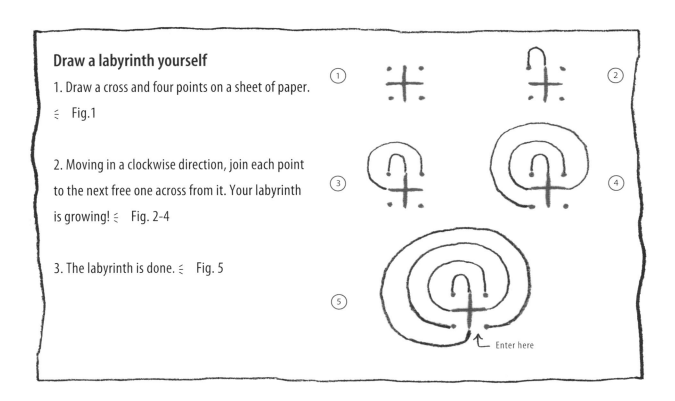

① ② ③ ④ ⑤

Enter here

Large labyrinths were built in parks or churches so that people could stroll through them.

People who were troubled or hopeless were supposed to be able to find faith in life again.

The Maze

A maze and a labyrinth look very similar. The big difference is that here, you really can get lost. Many paths branch off and lead nowhere. Only one path leads to the goal.

This scatterbrained pirate has lost his treasure map. **Can you lead him to the island where his treasure lies?** Which path does he have to take? Trace the right path with a pencil and solve the puzzle.

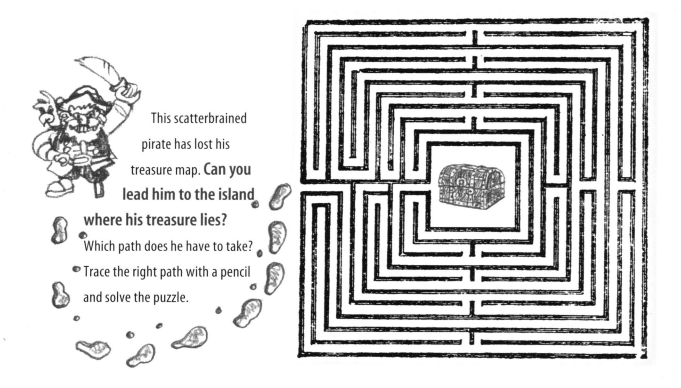

Since mazes are usually built of hedges, every path looks the same. Everywhere you look, only leaves, leaves, leaves, and eventually you lose your sense of direction. If you choose the wrong way, you find yourself standing in a dead end. You have to turn around and go back. Soon you no longer know where you are. People have always loved this kind of thrill.

In this ancient Greek myth you'll learn a good trick to help you find your way out of a maze.

The Legend of Ariadne's Thread

A long time ago, there was a man-eating monster, the Minotaur, who lived on the island of Crete. He was half man and half bull and lived in a maze. To keep him in there, each year the people of Athens offered him seven young men and seven maidens. The parents, of course, wept bitterly when their daughter's or son's lot was drawn. So the hero Theseus decided to volunteer and to make a quick end of the Minotaur. After arriving in Crete, he met the king's daughter. They fell in love and forged a plan together. When it was Theseus' turn to be sacrificed to the Minotaur, Ariadne hid a sword and a large ball of red yarn at the entrance of the dark maze. Theseus attached one end of the thread to the entrance. He grabbed the sword and set off to kill the monster. As he walked, he unraveled the thread. Every time he lost his way in the maze, he simply followed the thread back. With this trick he was able to find the Minotaur and conquer him. To get back safely he only had to rewind the red thread. At the entrance Ariadne was waiting for him and the two fell happily into each other's arms.

Have you ever heard someone say that they've lost the thread of a story when they can't remember or follow along? It's lucky this didn't happen to Theseus. He was able to pick up the thread again after his fight.

Theseus fights the Minotaur in the maze

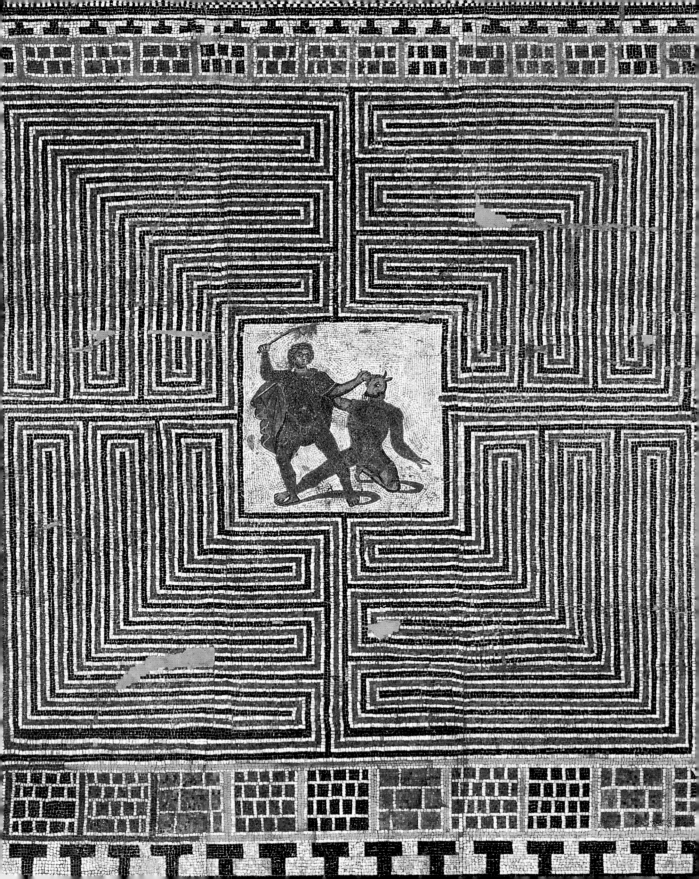

Modern Gardens

Today every possible kind of garden and park exists. Parks and gardens used to be reserved for the rich and powerful and their guests. Today many people can have their own small gardens. They plant flowers and trees or build swimming pools for themselves. Cities or other communities often own vast areas; there, parks are sometimes set up so that everyone can visit for fresh air and recreation. Whether a park is really still nature is an interesting question. Paths and beds for plants that have been laid out by people are not really natural or original. They have been part of human culture - as you already know - for a very long time. Nature has been transformed by people in very many ways and there is less and less space for wilderness. The cities are growing larger and displacing nature.

But people still long for nature. Even in densely settled areas, many try to plant greenery in a tiny plot of wasteland. Around forty years ago people joined together for the first time to make their cities more natural and more livable. They did not like how the city planners and politicians cemented over more and more of the urban areas. They demonstrated against it. But since no one seemed to take them seriously they decided to become active, and they founded the Guerilla Gardeners (guerillas are

people who fight independently and in secret for their cause). Armed with shovels, watering cans, and seeds, today they still plant greenery on vacant lots in the city. What they do doesn't hurt anyone! Maybe you can also find a small plot of nature in the city that no one takes care of. If you want to, you can adopt the plot and take care of it yourself.

Sometimes large areas of a city stand empty for many years. The owner may have built fences around them so that no one can get in, which is his right to do. In such areas, there's often trash lying around or rusty nails that could hurt someone. But the guerilla gardeners have even found a way to grow plants in these spaces. They make seed balls and throw them over the fences. Then they let nature do the rest.

You can find out more about guerilla gardening and seed balls on the website www.gruenewelle.org

If there's an abandoned lot near where you live and you want to help nature out a bit, there are instructions on how to make a seed ball on page 85.

Planted wall

Sometimes modern garden designers also have to be inventive to bring more greenery into the city. When no level areas are available, they use walls and facades.

Artists' Gardens

Many artists have designed and built up large gardens. These are creative and imaginative works that combine different kinds of art. Here are a couple of examples.

Spoerri Garden in Tuscany, Italy

In the Italian region of Tuscany, the Swiss artist Daniel Spoerri found a lovely spot for realizing his idea for a garden. You can stroll for hours here through the large garden, between olive trees and through meadows of flowers, and come across small and large sculptures. Some are by Daniel Spoerri himself, and others were made by artist friends of his. You can take a virtual tour of the Spoerri Garden at www.danielspoerri.org

Tarot Garden by Niki de Saint Phalle, Tuscany, Italy

The artist Niki de Saint Phalle also built a garden in Tuscany – her Tarot Garden. She was fascinated by the figures on Tarot cards, which people use to tell fortunes. Her sometimes enormous creations are like a monument to these figures. Some of them are so large that you can walk into them; Niki even built her house in one of them.

You can see more images on the website, www.nikidesaintphalle.com

Gaudi`s Parc Güell in
Barcelona, Spain

In Spain, the architect Antonio Gaudí was commissioned to design a park in the city of
Barcelona. He wanted to deal with the site very sensitively and not drastically change the
landscape. So he adapted his plans to nature. Even the structures in the park are designed in
keeping with natural forms. They seem very modern; it is hard to believe that this park is
already over a hundred years old.

Land Art

For many people, digging around in their garden beds is the best possible recreation. Others prefer to fill their free time with outdoor games and sports, or just hanging around in a hammock.

Artists in nature are interested in more than simple recreation. They are alert and curious, and their art is a reaction to life. They pose questions to themselves and to us. These questions are not simple ones like: What time is it, please? Do you also have this shirt in green? Is this the way to the skating rink? Instead, artists ask: What should the future look like? What do you need in order to be happy? Is there more to life than just what our eyes can see? These questions are a bit more tricky and don't offer any easy solutions. Works of art are meant to make us pay attention and listen. The works of artists invite us to marvel at them.

Around forty years ago, artists began to work with nature in a completely new way than their predecessors had. They did not lay out gardens and parks; they didn't want to make everything nice and comfortable. These were the Land Art artists.

To understand more about such artists and art, it is helpful to know about the time in which the artists lived. You can ask yourself: What was going on back then? What did the artists experience? You can then understand better what the artists were reacting to and why they asked the questions they did. If we want to know why and how the Land Art movement came about, we'll have to crank up our time machine and return to the past, to America in the 1960s.

Reality Check

We often think we know what something feels like or sounds like without even trying it. Try finding things when you are walking outside with friends, and then describe how you think they will feel or smell or what they will sound like: cool or warm, dry or wet, soft or rough, perfumed or stinky. Then do a reality check. Feel with your hands or your whole body, listen carefully, and smell. Is it really like what you thought it would be? Can you now find the right words to describe it?

The terrible Second World War had been over for twenty years. People had hope again in a better and more peaceful future. And they also wanted to enjoy life a bit. The economy was booming, products were churned out nonstop. If people needed more furniture, forests were razed to get the wood. If cars were needed, then more drilling was done to produce the oil to run them. People wanted to buy more and more things and buy them cheaply. And the smokestacks of the factories coughed out smoke.

These were turbulent times. Many young people disliked how politics and the society were developing. For even though the horrors of the Second World War were deeply etched in people's memories, American soldiers were being sent off to fight again in a new war, this time in Vietnam.

The youth saw their parents' and grandparents' generation as strict, eager for war, superficial, and unfeeling. They longed for peace, love, freedom, and closeness to nature. One of their slogans was "make love, not war." As a sign of this, some of them let their hair grow long and wore flowers in it. Many painted their cars bright colors and danced to wild music. Many were upset about the destruction of the environment and founded organizations like Greenpeace to protect it.

Artists of the time had become tired of their artworks not stimulating people to ask questions, but merely being bought by collectors - as cars, shoes, or slices of pizza were. They thought that works of art should not be "consumed" mindlessly.

But what could they do?

The first Land Art artists decided to make works of art that were so large, they couldn't be collected by people. They chose the landscape as their new sphere. Art should not only be free, it should also be done out in the open. Whoever wanted to see it would have to take a long trip. And instead of high heels and silk ties, at the opening of these exhibitions you were better off in rubber boots and a windbreaker. And - hooray - the first questions were raised immediately: Do I really want to drive so far? Is art worth it to me?

Robert Smithson,
Spiral Jetty, 1970

There are many impressive works of Land Art. Here you'll be introduced to some of them. One of the first and most important was made by Robert Smithson in America: Spiral Jetty.

For this Earthwork, earthmovers dug up and transported 6,500 tons of soil and stone! The Jetty is a spiral almost 450 yards long and 4 yards wide.

When Robert Smithson went to the Great Salt Lake in Utah for the first time, the land seemed to waver. In his imagination water and earth were swirling together. He felt like he was moving on solid ground, even though the water seemed completely still. He used the form of a spiral to represent this merging of the solid and fluid. Like the labyrinth, the spiral is also a symbol for life. Here the water ebbs and flows with the tides. He realized that his giant sculpture could disappear with time. Two years later the water level of the Great Salt Lake rose. Since then the spiral has not been visible. So has the work of art actually been destroyed? What do you think? Isn't it nice - and mysterious - to think that a work of art lies beneath the surface of the water?

The Secret

You can share a secret wish or a secret worry with nature. When something in your life becomes too much to handle, find a couple of stones along the shore somewhere: large stones for large worries or wishes, small stones for small ones. Hold each stone squarely in your hand and recite everything that troubles you. Then throw them as far as you can into the water. They will take your thoughts with them to the bottom, lightening your load for you.

The American artist Michael Heizer also had the earth moved in order to make his ideas visible. The picture to the left shows one such work of art.

This angular line of ditches was located in the Nevada desert. After only two weeks it was eroded by wind and weather and soon disappeared. What remains are photographs and memories.

Michael Heizer,
Nine Nevada
Depressions,
Rift #1,
Jean Dry Lake,
Nevada, 1968

What do you think? Can the Earth also remember things? How long will our traces be visible? These are questions that occupied the English artist Richard Long. Many of his works were produced while he was hiking. They make his reflections and questions visible. He produced lines by walking, for example. He walked up and down a field over and over again, arriving nowhere, of course. But his movements remained visible in the grass for a while. Walking has become a part of his art. Aren't we usually trying to get somewhere, reach some distant goal, when we move? Why didn't Richard Long do this? His goal was the exploration of time and the landscape. And he reached this goal without moving very far at all.

The picture above looks funny, as if the cars had fallen from the sky. They are Cadillacs, cars that used to be considered special symbols of America's technological progress. But what did the tree artists Chip Lord, Hudson Marquez, and Doug Michels of the artists' group Ant Farm want to show with this? It also looks a little bit like a graveyard. But what has been buried here? To understand the idea, imagine these aren't Cadillacs but the latest video game consoles, the newest cell phones, or the coolest clothes.

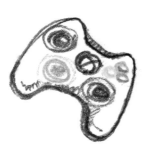

Nancy Holt made the artwork Sun Tunnels out of concrete pipes in the Utah desert. When you go in, you can see that different holes have been drilled in each of the six-meter-long tunnels. Light falls through the holes into the dark tunnel, forming constellations on the ground. The sun, whose light makes it impossible to see the stars during the day, simulates the stars and brings the heavens down to earth for us.

You can also cast constellations on the wall.

Read how on page 86!

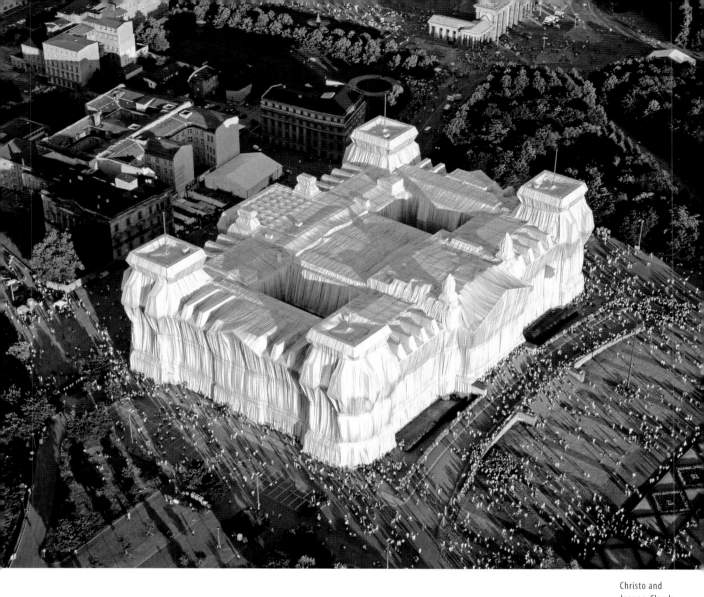

When it's your birthday, you surely get presents that are nicely wrapped. You're happy and very curious about unpacking what's inside.

The artist couple Christo and Jeanne-Claude wrapped entire coastlines, islands, trees, large buildings, and much more. When things that you have seen a thousand time are suddenly hidden, it makes you curious again. When the veil is lifted, you see the object with new eyes.

Nature Art

Over time, the ideas that artists wanted to express and explore in nature changed. Land Art artists sought to bring art into the landscape. Another group of artists were interested in nature itself. They developed Environmental Art.

Nature artists very often work with what they find right in front of them, such as leaves, grass, branches, flowers, light, and water. But these materials wilt or dissolve - such is the nature or nature! For this reason many of these works now exist only in the form of photographs. Others, made of sturdier materials like stone or rock, survive longer.

Through their art, the nature artists want to get to know nature very well and understand it. To do so, they carefully and intentionally observe every color and form. They feel the wind, the sun, and the rain. They attentively listen to sounds. For them, forms, colors, and tones tell the story of the place and the time. Their works give a visible form to their study of the natural world. They collect impressions and experiences and in this way come closer to the miracle of nature.

Vantage point

Try to find an old, empty picture frame in the attic or at a flea market. Take it with you when you go outdoors into nature. Hold it in front of you with outstretched arms and look through it. Pay careful attention to what you can see. If you turn around, the frame will show you another picture. If you hold it against the ground, you see something different than when you hold it up to the sky. You can even play this as a game with some friends. Notice carefully what you've seen and describe it to the others. They can then use the frame to try and to find your vantage point. Take turns so that everyone can try.

How can you swap ideas with something that uses no words, like nature? Each artist finds his or her own answer to this question. That's also why each work of art is so personal and unique. Let's take a look at what different artists have discovered about form, color, water, air, space, time, and humankind.

FORM

Artists explore forms in nature or give a shape to things that are invisible. Sometimes they surprise us with soft curves in a hard material. Other times they make small things very, very large - so that we look more carefully at these small things the next time we see them.

Birds' nests are often hidden high up in the branches of trees, so that the chicks are safe from predators. Artist Nils-Udo recreated a nest, but much larger. This nest is so large that you could even slide in yourself.

Nils-Udo, The Nest,
earth, stones, birch, grass,
Luneburg Heath, Germany,
1978, ilfochrome on
aluminium, 124 x 124 cm

My Nest
Birds build nests so that their chicks are safe and warm and can grow up comfortably. Imagine that you're a baby bird. What should your nest be like? At home in your room you can build a cozy little place for yourself. Collect everything soft and cuddly and design your nest. If you peep as loudly as a baby bird, maybe someone will bring you a worm!

In this artwork, Andy Goldsworthy has tried to make the invisible visible for us. In his imagination, the roots of the two trees intertwine into a tangled network. Can you see in this picture whether the two trees are connected or separate? What do you think? Do we humans also have invisible roots in nature that bind us to it tightly?

Andy Goldsworthy made tree roots of sand.

All throughout the forest there are underground waterways. When they emerge on the surface we can see them in the form of springs or streams. In this work of art by Diana Lynn Thompson, it seems as if the pinecones form a whirlpool and will float away any minute. Can you figure out the direction? Are the pinecones flowing into the ground or bubbling out of it?

Diana Lynn Thompson, On my Knees, 2004

Color works by
Andy Goldsworthy

COLOR

What color do you think of when you think of nature? Perhaps brown like soil, green like leaves, and blue like the sky? But all colors occur in nature, even strong and loud ones. Just think of the brilliant coloration of tropical fish, butterflies, or gemstones.

Just how many shades of color surround us everyday becomes clear when we arrange them in an unusual way. Only then can their brilliance become clear. When the artist Andy Goldsworthy works with colors, what he makes is so astonishing and impressive that you might mistakenly think he is a magician.

How many colors can you find in nature?

Read more on page 86!

Water

Water can be solid or liquid, and when it's hot it evaporates. Water has different qualities in each of the different states. As solid ice it is cold, hard, and rigid; in liquid form it can flow, reflect, and take the form of anything that contains it; and as gaseous steam it is hot, light, and floats in the air. For these reasons, water is a fascinating material for artists.

Look how the leaves are mirrored here in the calm surface of a lake. It looks as if another whole world existed underwater.

Nils-Udo, Robinia Leaf Swing: robinia leaves halved, ash twigs, Valle de Sella, Italy, 1992, ilfochrome on aluminium, 124 x 124 cm

Liquid water comes out of a shower.

Solid ice water can form into icicles.

Gaseous steam occurs when water is boiled at a high temperature.

Would you like to know how to make the current of a body of water easily visible?

Find out on page 87!

For the Persian artist Ahmad Nadalian, fish are symbols of the **human soul**. They are thirsty for life. Like a shaman in earlier times or a good pastor today, Nadalian wants to help people. He engraves the fish onto stones and then returns them to nature once again, where they can become vigorous and swim like **fish in water**.

Ahmad Nadalian,
Fish Stones
in Water

Ice work by Andy
Goldsworthy

Look at the picture to the left. You need a sure instinct, a delicate touch, and a lot of experience with ice to create such a wonderful and **fragile work** of art. When the sunlight hits the artwork, it begins to sparkle and shine like a jewel. But soon the warmth causes the ice to melt back into water and return to its source.

How do you make frozen pictures?

Read how on page 87!

Air

Although we need air to breathe, we are seldom aware of its presence. For we can see air only when it sweeps across the land as wind and causes something to move. We notice the wind when it whips against our cheeks as a cold gale or when it brings sweet scents to our nose. Perhaps we need special antennas to be able to feel the air better. As fine and delicate as feathers, these antennas would let us sense even the slightest breath of wind - just like the fluttering artwork shown at the end of the book, which is by Kari Joller.

Read about it on page 88!

The wind is playful. It swirls the leaves around the ground, tousles our hair, and blows sailboats across the water. Would you like to make the wind something special, a surprise?

The royal pair float through the air, weightless and almost invisible. When the barometric pressure falls, they deflate. But until then they can dance like mad, letting themselves be carried and lifted by the wind. Enchanted, we can applaud each of their elegant pirouettes.

Space

Now here are artworks that exist in grand spaces! Each of the works' artists has found a different way to give us a feeling of size and v a s t n e s s in nature. For one can easily claim that nature is the largest thing we know. It extends even to the sky and beyond. Have you ever flown in an airplane? From up there, you have a very special view of our world. The houses look small, like dollhouses. Great forests look like the fur of a giant green teddy bear. Lakes look like splashes of water that someone spilled while walking by.

You can also experience the size and vastness of nature through works of art. In the work shown below, Mikael Hansen has cut a swathe through the forest. This path through nature is as straight as an arrow made of sticks. Where is it likely to end?

Mikael Hansen,
Organic Highway,
Tickon, Langeland,
Denmark, 1995

Jim Denevan's artworks take up a lot of space (it's good that nature is so large).
Using a broom and a rake he "draws" giant, geometric patterns in the sand, which exist only
briefly. At high tide, the water washes the pictures into the sea. Without a photograph,
only the memories of the artist and the sand remain.

Time

Nature is ceaselessly changing. When the sun rises in the morning, the birds awake and the flowers open. In the evening it is cooler, and the time arrives for a concert of crickets or frogs. Life blossoms and flourishes and then withdraws as the seasons change. Art that is made from living nature also flourishes and then dies away, like this house. In the winter it shows us its ribs, and in summer it reveals it´s best dress of foliage.

Carlotta Brunetti,
Clover House
in February,
EXPO 2000

Carlotta Brunetti,
Clover House in
May, EXPO 2000

Would you like to get to know your "meadow self"?

*Read about it
on page 88!*

This work is called Raincatcher. The artist built it in the forest to visually show how everything is transformed through time and life. You can see in this work how nature slowly occupies it, overruns it, and ultimately dissolves it. But until then, it looks beautiful and even a bit ghostly.

Diana Lynn Thompson, Raincatcher, 2005

Man

The earth and nature are our actual home. We humans are made out of the same materials as they are. Water, earth, and energy are the building blocks of our bodies, and at the end of our lives we dissolve into them once again.

Nils-Udo,
water nest,
Chiemgau, Bavaria,
Germany, 2001,
ilfochrome
on aluminium,
100 x 100 cm

The Earth bears us and, since we move upon it, we leave behind our tracks. The footprints in this work of art are golden, as if an angel had walked across the water.

Carlotta Brunetti,
"An angel step
across the water…"

Ahmad Nadalian,
Hidden Treasures

As part of his art, Ahmad Nadalian buries his creations all around the world in holes in the ground. People who observe him doing it may secretly want to retrieve the "treasure," hoping to find gold and jewels. But at the bottom of each hole there is only a simple stone with a motif carved into it. These stones are the treasure, though people often do not realize it. For the carved stones represent the artist's ideas and good wishes for the whole earth.

The Earth and nature are inconceivably rich in **form,** color, space, and time. This fact can be frightening, especially if you think, "How large nature is, and how small I am in comparison." But we don't need to be afraid, for we too are all part of nature. We are as large as the universe and as small as a grain of sand. Just as the leaves let their colors shine, we too can breathe poetry into life.

Diana Lynn Thompson,
writing poetry on leaves,
2000/2001

In order to comprehend and fathom nature better, many attempt to measure, count, and describe it. But in its essence nature remains a miracle. In order to make this clear to us, Diana Lynn Thompson and some helpers individually numbered each leaf on a tree. What do you think: Will the sum of the leaves still be correct a week later?

Diana Lynn Thompson,
hundreds+thousands,
2000/2001

Nature in the Gallery

When you roam through nature, you surely can find lots of great things to put in your pocket and take home with you: stones with a special pattern, a knotty piece of wood, regularly-shaped pine cones, flowers, leaves, or any number of other objects. When you look at your "booty" more carefully once you're home, you'll certainly discover more that you hadn't noticed at first - beautiful forms and surfaces, patterns and shades of colors. Maybe even an ant or some other small animal has smuggled his way inside.

Objects from nature change when they are removed from their environment. When you take stones out of the water, their colors fade; plants dry out when plucked from the soil; and wood picked up from the ground becomes brittle or rotten. Artists have found unusual ways to bring nature or experiences of nature into the museum. In contrast to nature, a museum exhibition space is small and you sense immediately that it is not natural. There, you're not distracted by bird songs or the scent of tree resin. In this man-made environment, it is sometimes possible to get a much clearer view of nature and discover unfamiliar sides of it.

Over the next few pages, you can see some of these artists' works.

My little gallery

To design your own little gallery, you'll need empty glass jars - such as jelly jars - and a place where you can display them so that they can be seen easily. Begin collecting your pieces next time you go out. Place each one in a glass. Think about how you would like to arrange and label the glasses. What does a visitor to your exhibition learn about your trip outside or your local area? Do your objects tell a kind of story? You can also think of specific themes for your gallery; themes such as summer, or your way to school, or your favorite stones. Choose anything you like!

Olafur Eliasson
Beauty, 1993
Spotlight, water,
nozzles, wood,
hose, pump
Dimensions variable

The famous Icelandic artist Olafur Eliasson works closely with natural elements such as water, light, and color - even within interior spaces! Eliasson's art mixes up our ideas about art and nature. He makes the colors of the rainbow appear before our eyes on a curtain of fog in the middle of a room, and it looks like magic.

In a condemned house in Vienna, the Italian artist Letizia Werth has designed a garden of dust flowers. It is an image of dying and renewal in nature. In a dying house this unusual garden recalls nature's rhythms. But the fact that these creations are not simply flower pots containing real plants can make you think: Where is the life in these flowers?

Letizia Werth,
Dust Flower Garden,
Vienna, 2004

Aurora Robson takes a very different path. By working with old plastic bottles, she makes plastic into art. Environmental protection is very important to the artist. For her lush artificial landscapes, she uses materials that others consider trash. Doesn't this work seem to resemble a jungle or living bodies?

Aurora Robson,
Installation,
The Great Indoors,
Rice Gallery,
Houston, Texas, 2008

Levi van Veluw,
Landscapes,
2008

In these works, Levi van Veluw not only
has nature in his head, but also on it!
The pictures are a very unusual kind of
self-portrait. They remind us that
people are a part of nature and nature
is a part of people.

Farewell

Now you have reached the end of your hike through this book. Your path led you through gardens and parks, and it showed you how people design their environments. You were able to raise questions along with artists and become acquainted with their views of nature.

You have dug your way through, layer by layer, and gotten to know some of nature's most beautiful aspects. You found yourself in a labyrinth, played with the wind, arranged colors, and much more. When you go through life with your senses keen and alert, you will discover many wonderful things all by yourself, for nature and life are endless and you are a part of them.

Interested in a Little Field Trip?

So now you've had a chance to read about and look at a lot of art and nature, and you've already learned a great deal about them. Now you can take some time to stroll through old gardens or modern sculpture parks and listen to the chirping of birds! Would you like to find out how it feels to be in the passageways of a labyrinth or smell the delightful scent of a rose or herb garden? Yes? Then what are you waiting for?!

Do you live in California? Then perhaps you already know Niki de Saint Phalle's sculpture garden in San Diego called Queen Califia's Magical Circle. Do you live in England? England is famous for its gardens and parks!

Wherever you live, or wherever you travel, there are surely chances to visit artfully designed landscapes, works of nature art, or artist's gardens. The best way to find out would be to do some Internet research and then ask your parents if they would be interested in joining you on an art-and-nature field trip.

Ideas for Creative Projects,

Games,

and Discoveries

Daisy soup

Read about it on page 7

You'll need: two handfuls of daisies (without stems), one quart of vegetable broth, one small onion, one large potato, 2 tablespoons of butter, and a little cream. To season it you'll need salt, pepper, and nutmeg.

How to make it: Wash the daisies and chop finely, reserving a couple to garnish the finished soup. Peel and chop the onion and potato. Melt the butter in a pot and briefly saute the remaining ingredients. Then pour in the vegetable broth and let the soup simmer for ten minutes. Remove the pot from the heat, stir in the cream, and use a blender to puree the soup. After you have filled the soup bowls, garnish them with a couple of the left-over daisies. Enjoy!

A bean (almost) as fast as a rocket

Read about it on page 12

If you would like to garden sometime without having to wait too long, then runner beans (or scarlet runner beans) are a good choice. Collect a couple of dried beans and flower pots filled with good soil. Press each bean an inch deep into the soil and then set the pots in a warm and light place. Don't forget to water them! The first green shoots can be seen in only four to five days. They grow very quickly and will soon need a pole on which to climb. If you take good care of them, they will soon surprise you with beautiful red blossoms. If they grow pods with beans in them, please don't eat them raw. They are delicious only when cooked; when raw they are toxic.

Cave painting

Read about it on page 16

To make a cave painting, you´ll have to produce the paints yourself. For pigment you'll need dried, powdered soil. You can gather it on a walk and then sift it. If you pay close attention, you'll notice that there are different types of soils. Their colors differ; some are brown, others gray, still others yellowish. The more colors you find, the more colorful your pictures can be.

Mixing: First the base is made. It consists of equal amounts of egg, oil, and water. Stir the three ingredients together. Then add just enough sifted soil to make a fine paste. You can use this paste to paint with. As a canvas, you'll need a rock wall or a large stone. You can apply the paint with a bristle brush or a twig. Try to depict a scene from your daily life, like the earliest cave painters did.

Amazing

Read about it on page 19

Do you believe that you can change the colors of flowers? Try it. Take some cut flowers with white blossoms, for example white roses. You can put them in a vase of water with blue or green ink in it. After only a short time you can see how the flower petals take on the color of the water. You can even slice the stem lengthwise into two long strips. Put each strip of stem into a glass with a different-colored water. You'll see how, for example, one half of the flower turns blue and the other green.

Miniature paradise

Read about it on page 23

For your own little paradise, you'll need a plastic tub about four to five inches deep. To keep the soil from rotting, place an inch of Leca clay balls in the bottom. The soil is placed on top of them, and it should reach to about a half inch below the rim of the tub. Now you can plant your little paradise any way you want. When you're done, you can place a few of your toy figures into the new paradise. Don't forget to water and take care of your tiny garden.

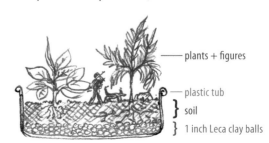

plants + figures

plastic tub

} soil

} 1 inch Leca clay balls

Scented pictures

Read about them on page 25

To make a spice picture, you'll need colorful spices from the store, for example red paprika powder, yellow turmeric, green oregano, brown fennel and linseed, star anise…

On a sturdy piece of cardboard, use a pencil to draw a simple picture with different parts to it. Now choose one of the parts of the picture to cover thickly with glue. Then scatter the spice onto the glue. Let it dry a while before you decorate the next part. Step by step you will make a picture that is not only beautiful to look at, but also gives off a wonderful aroma.

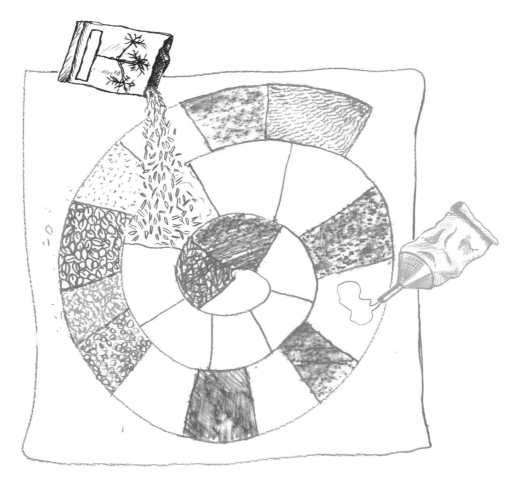

Water games

Read about them on page 27

On a hot, sunny day during summer vacation, you can tackle a large project: your own water park for you and your friends. In case you don't have a yard, ask a friend if you can do it in his or hers. Here are a couple of ideas for things you can do with water.

Water gun course: Armed with water pistols, form two lines facing each other. The most courageous one among you starts and runs between the lines while the rest unload everything they have. Then it's the next one's turn.

Water slide: Lay a long and sturdy piece of plastic sheeting on the ground (you can buy it in a home improvement store). Spray it with a hose until it's very wet. Then take a running start and fling yourself along the plastic at full speed.

Fountain figure: You and your friends can make yourselves into a fountain. Just like with the fountains of the old masters, here you'll become the statues that represent gods or mermaids. Before you take a photo of the finished fountain, grab a garden hose that is spouting water - and voilà, the work of art is finished.

Bobbing for apples: You will need a large tub or thick plastic container for water. Fill it to the top with water and put some apples in it. Then, not using hands, each child in turn must try to get an apple from the water with his or her mouth and take a bite. Have fun!

Swimthingies: Blow up a plastic wading pool and fill it with water. Then, on land, you can make unusual things out of pieces of bark, old plastic bottles, Styrofoam, and other materials that float, and let them sail away in the wading pool.

Water candles: In the evening when it gets dark, lighting your own homemade floating candles looks very pretty. To make them you'll need nutshells, wicks, and modeling wax.

Form a small candle, with a wick in the center, out of the modeling wax and press it into the nutshell. An adult should light the candles. Together, you can set them on the water in a bowl or in the tub where you had bobbed for apples.

Seed Balls

Read about it on page 39

To keep a seed from being washed away by the rain or eaten by birds, you have to build it a protective cover.

You'll need:

• various dried seeds from regional wildflowers, herbs, or vegetables

• good potting soil

• dry red or brown clay powder (not wet clay from the craft store)

• some water

Proportions: 1 part seeds, 4 parts soil, 4 parts clay powder

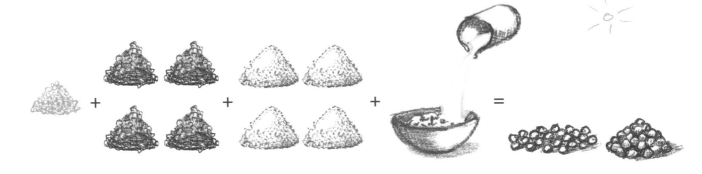

Instructions: First, mix the seeds well with the soil. Then mix in the dry clay. Finally, carefully add just enough water so that the mass sticks together. You can now begin to form small balls, about the size of hazelnuts. Place them in the sun for a day or two until they are dry. Now the first seed balls are finished, and you can set out to release them!

Constellations

Read about it on page 52

There are twelve signs of the zodiac in the Western horoscope. Do you know under which one you were born? These twelve, as well as many more, are in fact constellations in the sky. Choose a constellation from a star chart and transfer the pattern of the stars onto the inside of a shoebox by drawing a point for each star; then poke little holes through the points. When it is dark in your room at night, hold the perforated side of the box towards a wall and shine a flashlight through it. You can then see your constellation on the wall.

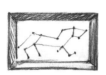  

Finding the colors in nature

Read about it on page 57

In the spring, when the flowers bloom, the fields take on bright color. In the fall, it's the leaves of the trees and the amazing light that transforms the color of everything. If you want to find out which colors occur during a particular season, collect flower petals or leaves and sort them by color. Create a sequence of colors like the one in the rainbow or in a new box of colored pencils - maybe arranging them from light to dark.

See how water moves

Read about it on page 58

You can make the current of a stream visible by making a chain of leaves. Attach several leaves, one next to the other, to a string by tying each of their stems firmly. When your leaf chain is about six feet long, you can place it in the water to float. Its movements will always follow the current. But it should only float slowly. If it floats too fast, the chain will be gone before you've seen anything ...

Art for ice-cold days

Read about it on page 59

To record a picture in water, you can freeze it. Collect a couple of beautiful, flat objects - such as leaves, thin twigs, grasses, or individual flower petals. Fill a flat-bottomed plastic container with a half inch of water and leave it in the freezer until it has turned into solid ice. Or, if it's under 32° outside, you can put the container outdoors overnight. Next, using the objects you collected, make a picture on the layer of ice. Cover the picture with water and freeze it again. When everything is frozen solid, you can loosen the picture from the container. If it doesn't come out easily, let a little warm water flow over the container until the picture comes loose. Since the picture will melt in the house, bring it quickly outside where it's cooler. It's especially nice if, in the evening, you put a candle behind it and illuminate the ice picture from behind. As is common with nature art, it will only last so long. But that's only natural.

Wind Catcher

Read about it on page 60

To make a wind catcher, you'll need a frame or a tire that can be hung up from the top. Below, you can tie on feathers and leaves or string flowers or cotton balls together. If you tie little bells onto the frame, you can always hear when the wind is growing stronger - which is the best time to watch your creation move and flutter about!

Meadow self

Read about it on page 64

Buy a sturdy piece of plastic sheeting from the home improvement store. It should be at least as long as you are tall. Lay the sheet on the floor at home. Lie down on it and have someone trace your outline on the plastic sheet with a pen or masking tape. Then cut out the form: Now you have the shape of your body in plastic. Find a well-mowed patch of grass and lay your "plastic self" out on it. You'll have to weigh it down with some stones so it won't get blown away by the wind. Now you only need a little patience, for your "meadow self" will become visible in the grass after only a few days.

Barbara Stieff lives and
works in Vienna as a
freelance author, director,
and cultural educator.
www.barbarastieff.at
Photo © Judith Dolleschka

© Prestel Verlag, Munich · London · New York, 2011

© for reproductions of works by the artists or their heirs with the exception of: Robert Smithson, Nancy Holt,
Carlotta Brunetti, Letizia Werth: VG Bild-Kunst, Bonn 2011; Michael Heizer: Triple Aught Foundation; p. 51: ©1974
by Ant Farm (Lord, Marquez, Michels) ; p. 53 ©1995 Christo; p. 71: © 1993 Olafur Eliasson, Courtesy the artist;
neugerriemschneider, Berlin; and Tanya Bonakdar Gallery, New York

The Deutsche Nationalbibliothek lists this publication in the Deutsche Nationalbibliographie; detailed
bibliographic information is available at http://dnb.ddb.de.

Photo credits: All photographic material was kindly made available by the artists or has been taken from the
publisher's archives with the exception of:
Nash Baker: p. 74/75; Umberto Brayj: p. 39 oben; Judith Dolleschka: p. 89; Getty Images: p. 47;
D. Gorton: p. 48; Bobak Ha'Eri: p. 20; Jean-Luc Henry: p. 39 below; Hansueli Krapf: p. 4;
kreativo GbR Soiderer/Asenbeck: p. 79; Doris Kutschbach: frontispiece, p.12, 26, 28, 41, 42, 44, 45, 80; NASA: p. 8/9;
Niki Odolphie: p. 35; Poul Pedersen: p. 71; Photocase / m|ias: endpaper; Matti Piiroinen: p. 13; Wolfgang Volz: p. 53
All hand-drawn illustrations: Michael Schmölzl

Prestel Verlag, Munich
A member of the Verlagsgruppe Random House GmbH

www.prestel.com

Translation: Cynthia Hall
Project coordination: Doris Kutschbach
Editing: Brad Finger
Picture editing: Andrea Jaroni
Design: Michael Schmölzl, agenten.und.freunde, Munich
Production: Nele Krüger
Art Direction: Cilly Klotz
Lithography: Reproline mediateam, Munich
Printing and binding: Neografia, Martin

MIX
Paper from
responsible sources
FSC® C020353
FSC
www.fsc.org

Verlagsgruppe Random House FSC-DEU-0100
The FSC-certified paper Hello Fat Matt 1,1 has been
supplied by Condat, Le Lardin Saint-Lazare, France.

ISBN 978-3-7913-7048-4